# Stock Cars

By Denny Von Finn

Torque™

BELLWETHER MEDIA • MINNEAPOLIS, MN

Are you ready to take it to the extreme?
Torque books thrust you into the action-packed world of sports, vehicles, and adventure. These books may include dirt, smoke, fire, and dangerous stunts.
**WARNING:** read at your own risk.

This edition first published in 2011 by Bellwether Media, Inc.



Library of Congress Cataloging-in-Publication Data

Von Finn, Denny.
Stock cars / by Denny Von Finn.
p. cm. -- (Torque: the world's fastest)
Includes bibliographical references and index.
ISBN 978-1-60014-589-6 (hardcover : alk. paper)
Summary: "Amazing photography accompanies engaging information about stock cars. The combination of high-interest subject matter and light text is intended for students in grades 3 through 7"--Provided by publisher.
1. Stock cars (Automobiles)--Juvenile literature. I. Title.
TL236.28.V66 2010
796.72--dc22 2010034747



Printed in the United States of America, North Mankato, MN.

010111 1176

# CONTENTS


| | |
|---|---|
| What Are Stock Cars? | 4 |
| Stock Car Technology | 10 |
| The Future of Stock Cars | 16 |
| Glossary | 22 |
| To Learn More | 23 |
| Index | 24 |

# What Are Stock Cars?

Stock cars are race cars that excite fans with thrilling speeds. Stock car racing is popular in many countries around the world. The National Association for Stock Car Auto Racing (NASCAR) hosts nearly 40 races a year all over the United States. More than 200,000 fans go to some of the larger races.

## Fast Fact

**One lap around the longest NASCAR track is 2.66 miles (4.28 kilometers). The shortest track is just a 0.5 mile (0.8 kilometer) around.**

**Fast Fact**

**The noise made by a single stock car can measure 130 decibels. That's the same as a jet airliner passing just 100 feet (30 meters) overhead.**

Most stock car races are held on oval-shaped tracks. During a race, 43 cars speed around the track just inches from one another. Drivers **draft** behind other cars. This helps them maintain speed and save fuel.

Stock cars make an incredible amount of noise each time they pass the **grandstand**. Races are long, tough contests of 300 to 600 miles (483 to 966 kilometers). They require hundreds of laps.

Stock car racing began in the 1920s. Drivers raced old cars on dirt tracks. They removed parts to make their cars faster. Some people called these cars **jalopy racers**.

NASCAR formed in 1948 to make rules for stock car racing. Race cars had to be stock. This meant their engines and bodies could not be **modified**. These race cars were a lot like everyday family cars!

# Stock Car Technology

**Fast Fact**

The "headlights" on NASCAR stock cars are really stickers.

Modern stock cars are very complex. Strict rules tell race teams how to make the **body panels**. These metal pieces give stock cars a shape similar to everyday family cars. Underneath the body panels, however, modern stock cars are very different from cars seen on the street.

## Fast Fact

**The temperature inside a stock car during a race can reach 170 degrees Fahrenheit (76.7 degrees Celsius). A driver can sweat out 5 to 10 pounds (2.3 to 4.5 kilograms) in just one race.**

The body panels cover a **chassis**. This frame is made from strong steel tubes. The chassis includes a **roll cage** that protects the driver in case of a crash.

Important parts are connected to the chassis. The **suspension** helps the driver control the car around turns. Smooth tires attached to the suspension become hot and sticky during a race. This helps the stock car grip the track.

A stock car's large engine is mounted to the chassis. The engine has eight **cylinders** and is called a **V-8**. Four cylinders in each side of the engine form the shape of the letter "V." The engine can create 750 **horsepower**. That's almost four times more powerful than a typical car engine.

**Fast Fact**

Stock car engines get incredibly hot during a race. All of the parts of an engine need to be able to withstand extremely high temperatures.

213
213
C&R RACING RADIATORS

# The Future of Stock Cars

Stock car racing is expensive. New stock car technology helps racing teams save money. In the past, race teams had to build different stock cars for each type of track. NASCAR introduced the **Car of Tomorrow** in 2007. The Car of Tomorrow is designed to race on long and short tracks. Teams save money when they only need to build one kind of car.

24
GOODYEAR
Holley
3M
USG
TISSOT
JEGS
MOOG
MAHLE
COMP
Edelbrock
O'Reilly
Sprint

Recent stock car technology also helps the cars use less fuel. Every NASCAR engine had a **carburetor** until 2011. Now stock cars use **fuel injection**. Fuel injection requires less gasoline than a carburetor. Some drivers say fuel injection also makes the cars easier to drive.

Someday, stock cars might not use gasoline at all. More carmakers today are creating electric vehicles like the Chevy Volt.

Electric stock cars would only make **pit stops** for new tires. They would speed around the track with nearly silent electric motors!

# GLOSSARY

**body panels**—the brightly painted pieces of flat metal that cover a stock car

**Car of Tomorrow**—a stock car design introduced by NASCAR in 2007 to increase safety and decrease costs

**carburetor**—a device that mixes air and gasoline for an engine's cylinders

**chassis**—the frame on which a vehicle is built

**cylinders**—hollow chambers inside an engine in which fuel is burned to create power

**draft**—to closely follow another car to reduce air resistance and save fuel

**fuel injection**—a way in which fuel is pushed into an engine's cylinders

**grandstand**—the stands where fans sit to watch a stock car race

**horsepower**—a unit used to measure the power of an engine

**jalopy racers**—old cars that raced on dirt tracks in the 1920s and 1930s

**modified**—describes a vehicle that has been changed from its original form in order to go faster

**pit stops**—when cars pull off the track to re-fuel or get new tires

**roll cage**—a cage around the cockpit that protects the driver in case of a crash

**suspension**—the springs and shock absorbers that make a car easier for the driver to handle

**V-8**—an engine that has four slanted cylinders on each side that form a "V" shape

# TO LEARN MORE

## AT THE LIBRARY

David, Jack. *Stock Cars*. Minneapolis, Minn.: Bellwether Media, 2008.

Rashidi, Waleed. *NASCAR Learn to Draw Race Cars*. Minneapolis, Minn.: Walter Foster, 2006.

Roberts, Angela. *NASCAR's Greatest Drivers*. New York, N.Y.: Random House, 2009.

## ON THE WEB

Learning more about stock cars is as easy as 1, 2, 3.

1. Go to www.factsurfer.com.
2. Enter "stock cars" into the search box.
3. Click the "Surf" button and you will see a list of related Web sites.

With factsurfer.com, finding more information is just a click away.

# INDEX

1920s, 8
1948, 9
2007, 17
2011, 19
body panels, 11, 12
Car of Tomorrow, 17
carburetor, 19
chassis, 12, 13, 14
Chevy Volt, 20
cylinders, 14
drafting, 6
electric cars, 20, 21
fuel, 6, 19
fuel injection, 19
grandstand, 7
horsepower, 14
jalopy racers, 8
modification, 9
National Association for Stock Car Auto Racing (NASCAR), 5, 9, 10, 17, 19
noise, 6, 7
pit stops, 21
roll cage, 12
suspension, 13
temperatures, 12, 14
tires, 13, 21
tracks, 5, 6, 8, 13, 17, 21
United States, 5
V-8 engine, 14

The images in this book are reproduced through the courtesy of: Walter G. Arce, front cover, pp. 10-11, 12, 18-19; Jonathan Ferrey/Getty Images, pp. 4-5; Jerry Markland/Stringer/Getty Images, p. 6; Jamie Squire/Getty Images, p. 7; Archive Holdings Inc., p. 8; ISC Archives/Getty Images, p. 9; Matthew Jacques, p. 13; Sports Illustrated/Getty Images, pp. 14-15; Rusty Jarrett/Stringer/Getty Images, pp. 16-17; 6th Gear Advertising, pp. 20-21.